The Best Guide to Personal Growth Quotes and Ideas Book

Unlock Your Potential

By
Abigail Yeboah

Copyright © 2024 by Abigail Yeboah

All rights reserved.

No part of this book may be reproduced, stored in a retrieval system, or transmitted, in any form or by any means, electronic, mechanical, photocopying, recording, or otherwise, without the publisher's prior written permission.

Table of Contents

Chapter 1
Seeds of Transformation

Chapter 2
Planting the Mindset and Goal Set

Chapter 3
Nurturing Resilience

Chapter 4
Cultivating Self-Discovery

Chapter 5
Pruning Limiting Beliefs

Chapter 6
Fostering Growth Relationships

Chapter 7
Harvesting Gratitude and Mindfulness

Chapter 8
Sustaining Growth and Integration

Conclusion

Introduction

Picture yourself in front of a huge, beautiful garden. Verdant trees are reaching verdant trees reaching for the sun, colourful flowers dotting the scenery, and the pleasant aroma of possibilities permeating everything. Unleash your full potential in this garden. But it needs your entire focus, nurturing, and faith in its ability to flourish, just like any natural wilderness.

Learn how to nurture your own potential with the help of this book. "Unlock Your Potential: The Best Guide to Personal Growth Quotes and Ideas Book" goes beyond being a mere gathering of phrases and standard phrases. It serves as a guide, a compass, and a set of instruments for setting off on a life-altering adventure of learning and development.

First, it will look at what it takes to make a positive change, sowing the seeds of transformation. Developing a growth mentality that views obstacles as opportunities and failures as stepping stones. You will develop unfaltering emotional strength by learning to accept adversity and grow from your mistakes, which requires resilience.

The journey, however, is about more than simply surviving storms. Being oneself is the central theme. Together, set out on a trip to discover your potential abilities, values, and interests. Embrace the journey as you hack away at self-limiting ideas and plant the seeds of a growth mentality that will carry you far.

Prosperity never grows while unaccompanied. You have to cultivate mutually beneficial relationships to encourage and motivate one another. Rather than letting negative people drain your potential, you will learn to surround yourself with good people who will help you grow by teaching you how to set healthy boundaries and communicate effectively.

But one harvest is not the end of the road. Gratitude and mindfulness will be your guiding principles as you learn to appreciate the little things in life and use them to propel you forward. You will discover how to incorporate self-improvement into your everyday life, creating long-term patterns that feed your spirit and allow you to flourish season after season.

Always keep in mind that you possess limitless potential. With the help of this book, you may unlock the door to your garden, get your hands dirty, and see the incredible change waiting for you.

Chapter 1

Seeds of Transformation

Welcome to the beginning of your transformative journey. Within the pages of this book, you will discover the seeds of change, growth, and personal development. Each word, idea, and quote catalyze your evolution, guiding you towards unlocking your full potential and embracing the boundless possibilities that lie within.

Introduction to the Power of Personal Growth

Personal growth is not merely a journey but a profound exploration of self-discovery and empowerment. It is the recognition that within each of us lies the capacity to transcend our limitations, evolve beyond our current state, and become the architects of our destinies.

Personal growth is a lifelong journey of self-discovery and continuous improvement. It's about understanding yourself better, developing your skills and talents, and striving to become the best version of yourself. It encompasses various aspects of your life, including:

Emotional growth: Recognizing and managing your emotions, improving self-awareness, and building resilience.
Mental growth: Expanding your knowledge base, learning new things, and adopting a growth mindset.
Social growth: Strengthening relationships, practising effective communication, and fostering empathy.
Physical growth: Taking care of your health, developing healthy habits, and engaging in physical activity.
Spiritual growth: Exploring your values and beliefs, finding meaning and purpose in life.

Importance of personal growth:

Increased self-awareness: You gain a clearer understanding of your strengths, weaknesses, and values, leading to better decision-making.

Enhanced confidence and self-esteem: By working on yourself, you feel more capable and believe in your ability to achieve goals.

Improved relationships: Your communication and interpersonal skills blossom, leading to stronger and more fulfilling connections.

Greater resilience: You better handle challenges and bounce back from setbacks due to your developed coping mechanisms.

Achieving goals and dreams: Personal growth equips you with the skills and mindset necessary to pursue your aspirations.

Overall well-being and life satisfaction: By investing in yourself, you experience greater happiness, purpose, and fulfilment.

Personal growth is a personal journey, and its importance varies for each individual. **It's never too late or too early to start!** Remember, it's a continuous process with ups and downs, but the rewards are significant and enrich your life in various ways.

A critical part of bettering oneself is to adopt a new standard and enhance your way of life, concentrating on each area to see positive gains in your health. Your life's guiding principles encourage you to grow and develop yourself.

When you prioritize your physical, mental, emotional, and spiritual well-being, you can achieve all your dreams and realize your full potential. This is the first step on the road to self-improvement or personal growth.

There is a close relationship between the two; when you invest in these areas, your health will improve dramatically, allowing you to reach your full potential. Incorporate regular physical activity into your routine; begin with 30 minutes of light exercise and gradually increase the intensity.

It is crucial to consume a balanced diet that includes whole foods. As the saying goes, you are what you eat. In addition, if you want to improve your physical health, which is sure to affect your mental and emotional health, try drinking more water throughout the day. If you suffer from worry and stress, finding a method to reward yourself can help you feel better emotionally, mentally, and physically. It may seem exaggerated, but most people fail to recognize the significance of attending to their emotional and physical well-being; practising meditation may help both.

The power of personal growth resides in our ability to cultivate self-awareness, to challenge our beliefs and assumptions, and to embrace change as an opportunity for growth. Through this process of introspection and reflection, we begin to unearth our deepest desires, uncover our hidden talents, and unleash our true potential.

As you embark on this journey of personal growth, remember that it is not about reaching a destination but instead embracing the process of continual self-improvement. It is about embracing the discomfort of growth, stepping outside of your comfort zone, and embracing the challenges that come your way as opportunities for learning and development.

Exploring Foundational Principles for Self-Improvement

At the heart of personal growth lie foundational principles that serve as the building blocks for self-improvement. These principles encompass a commitment to lifelong learning, a willingness to take risks, and a dedication to personal accountability.

Lifelong learning is the cornerstone of personal growth, as it empowers us to expand our knowledge, broaden our perspectives, and embrace new ways of thinking. By cultivating a growth mindset and embracing a spirit of curiosity, we open ourselves up to endless possibilities for growth and transformation.

Taking risks is essential for personal growth, requiring us to step outside our comfort zones and embrace the unknown. We discover our strengths, confront our fears, and push past our limitations by taking risks. Each risk is an opportunity for growth and self-discovery, propelling us towards our fullest potential.

Personal accountability is the key to unlocking our power for change. It requires us to take ownership of our actions, accept responsibility for our choices, and commit to the ongoing process of self-improvement. By holding ourselves accountable, we empower ourselves to create the lives we desire and become our best versions.

Setting the Stage for a Transformative Journey

As you embark on this transformative journey, setting the stage for growth and change is essential. This requires a commitment to self-reflection, a willingness to embrace discomfort, and a readiness to let go of the familiar in pursuit of the extraordinary.

Self-reflection serves as the foundation for transformation, allowing us to examine our beliefs, values, and behaviours honestly and clearly. By reflecting on our experiences and learning from our mistakes, we gain valuable insights that guide us towards personal growth and self-discovery.

Embracing discomfort is a necessary part of the transformative process, as it challenges us to confront our fears, break free from our comfort zones, and embrace the unknown. We grow, evolve, and expand our horizons through discomfort, emerging stronger, wiser, and more resilient than before.

Letting go of the familiar is essential for transformation, as it allows us to release the old patterns, habits, and beliefs that no longer serve us. By letting go of the past and embracing the present moment, we create space for new opportunities, experiences, and possibilities to unfold.

As you embark on this journey of personal growth and transformation, remember that the seeds of change lie within you. It is up to you to nurture, cultivate, and watch them bloom into the fullest expression of your true potential.

"The only limits that exist are the ones you place on yourself." - Unknown.

"Your life does not get better by chance, it gets better by change." - Jim Rohn.

"The journey of a thousand miles begins with one step." - Lao Tzu.

"Success is not final, failure is not fatal: It is the courage to continue that count." - Winston Churchill.

"In the midst of movement and chaos, keep stillness inside of you." - Deepak Chopra.

Chapter 2:

Planting the Mindset And Goal Set

In the garden of personal growth, the mindset is the soil from which transformation blossoms. Understanding its significance, cultivating a growth-oriented perspective, and embracing challenges are essential to nurturing this fertile ground.

Your mindset is the lens through which you perceive the world and interpret your experiences. It shapes your beliefs, influences your actions, and ultimately determines your outcomes. Understanding the importance of mindset in personal growth is paramount to unlocking your full potential.

A fixed mindset sees abilities as static, leading to a reluctance to embrace challenges and a fear of failure. On the other hand, a growth mindset thrives on challenges, sees failure as an opportunity to learn, and believes in the power of effort to lead to mastery. Recognizing the impact of your mindset allows you to harness its power and direct it towards your growth journey.

By cultivating a growth-oriented perspective, you embrace the belief that your abilities can be developed through dedication and hard work. This shift in mindset opens the door to limitless possibilities, empowering you to overcome obstacles and achieve your goals.

Why goals are important: When you set goals to make your dreams come true, those goals become a road leading you to your end destination. This exercise can help clear your mind in many ways so that you can see clearly. You should set goals and keep track of your progress as you stick to your plan.

Setting goals forces you to take a break and recharge. Use these steps to make goal-setting work for you. Step one is, to be honest with yourself and ask yourself what you want from success. This will help you become more self-aware and determined. And because everyone has a different idea of what success means to them, yours will lead you differently than your friends. If you're unsure of your goals, you should start questioning yourself to discover your life's meaning.

Ask yourself things like, "What do I want to achieve? Where do I see myself in five years? What do I enjoy but could do better? How do I define success?" what are the things I can do that will help me move forward? These will allow you to figure out your goals and learn more about yourself. Don't overthink about it; write down the first answer that comes to mind. Remember that there are no right or wrong solutions. You will see a pattern emerge as you answer these questions individually. This pattern will be your committed way to creating or reshaping your goals.

Step 2: Put your goals in order of importance if you have many things you want to achieve. This will help you see your goals as real ones and understand why your life's goal can help you figure out what you desire. It could be getting your dream job, getting good grades in college, buying your first home, or having no debt. You don't have to aim for material things, of course. If you know what you want, you can also aim for happiness or peace of mind.

Third stage: If you write down your goals, you can see the steps you need to take to reach them more clearly. This will help your goals stick by leaving a mark on your mind. You can write them down and put them on your desk, in the mirror, front door, fridge, or anywhere else you can see them in your office or home. It will help you remember your main goal. And give you the drive and inspiration you need.

For instance, if your goal is to be financially independent because everyone has a different idea of financial freedom, you must make your own list. You have to write down your primary goal and then break it down into smaller steps. In this case, applying for your well-paid dream job will be the first thing you do to move closer to your goal. If you need to, break down your first milestone into even smaller steps and give yourself time to complete each.

Step 4: Set smart goals. Whether you're setting new goals for yourself in your daily life, studies, or career, your chances of success will depend on several factors. That's why you should set smart goals. For example, make sure your goals are clear. They should include the why, what, where, and how you will reach your goals.

Measurable: How will you know if you're reaching your goal? What checkpoints or steps will you use to see if you're doing that? Are you setting dates or keeping track of your progress as you grow? Write down a precise measurement that you can develop to track your progress toward your goals.

(A) it should be achievable; setting goals you can't reach is pointless, but that doesn't mean they should be easy. Set goals that are challenging but doable. If you don't, you'll waste your time and energy trying to reach a goal that you'll never get. This is also called being reasonable. Also, your goals should be attainable. Trying to picture a fantasy of hopes and dreams that will never come true is useless and hard to do.

In other words, be realistic and set goals you can reach.

(T) set time; make a schedule for each of your goals. You should be able to reach each goal within a certain amount of time. This will help you get all of your goals over the next few years within a clear and specific amount of time.

Step 5: Tell people you trust and believe about your goals. Many people will tell you not to tell anyone about your plans and goals for fear of jinxing them. Think about the opposite situation. If you speak to at least four people you trust and believe about your hopes and dreams, you will feel responsible for reaching your targets. Writing down, sharing, and discussing your goals creates a more precise picture for yourself.

That you need to be successful; this will also make you more determined to make your dreams come true. Reviewing, evaluating, and going over your goals again is the last thing you need to do to reach them. Keep an eye on your goals and your progress. Set a review date to check in on your work every week or month based on how much time you've given yourself. Setting goals is the first real thing you can do to improve yourself, and it will also keep you inspired and driven. It will make you plan and think intelligently about what you want to do with your life.

You have to be ready and willing to change no matter what. Because this will take a lot of hard work, determination, and persistence, you must promise to do the work and not stop until you meet your goal.

Cultivating a Growth-Oriented Perspective

Cultivating a growth-oriented perspective is about fostering resilience, embracing change, and adopting a continuous improvement mindset. It requires a willingness to step outside your comfort zone, confront challenges head-on, and view setbacks as opportunities for growth.

One way to cultivate a growth-oriented perspective is through the practice of reframing. Instead of seeing obstacles as roadblocks, see them as stepping stones to success. Embrace learning from failure, extracting lessons from setbacks, and using them to propel yourself forward.

Another essential aspect of cultivating a growth-oriented perspective is the practice of self-reflection. Take time to assess your progress, celebrate your successes, and identify areas for improvement. By staying curious and open-minded, you create space for growth and development in every aspect of your life.

Overcoming Obstacles and Embracing Challenges

Obstacles and challenges are an inevitable part of the personal growth journey. Instead of viewing them as barriers to success, see them as opportunities for growth and self-discovery. Embrace challenges with courage and resilience, knowing that overcoming each obstacle brings you one step closer to your goals.

Overcoming obstacles requires a mindset of perseverance and determination. It means staying committed to your vision, focused on your goals, and refusing to let setbacks derail your progress. Remember that the most significant achievements often arise from the greatest challenges; each obstacle you face is a chance to prove your strength and resilience.

Embracing challenges is not about avoiding discomfort but instead leaning into it with courage and conviction. It means pushing past your limits, confronting your fears, and embracing the unknown with an open heart and mind. By embracing challenges, you invite growth, transformation, and the fulfilment of your true potential into your life.

In the garden of personal growth, the mindset is the seed from which transformation blooms. By understanding its importance, cultivating a growth-oriented perspective, and embracing challenges, you nourish the soil of your mind, allowing the seeds of change to take root and flourish.

"Your mindset is the architect of your reality. Build wisely." - Unknown.

"In the garden of your mind, plant seeds of positivity, cultivate optimism, and reap the fruits of success." - Unknown.

"The mind is like a garden. What you plant, you grow. Choose your seeds wisely." - Unknown.

"A growth mindset is the key that unlocks the door to unlimited potential." - Carol S. Dweck.

"Obstacles are the raw materials of great accomplishments. Plant your mindset accordingly." - Unknown.

Chapter 3

Nurturing Resilience

Resilience is the cornerstone of personal growth, serving as the bedrock upon which we weather life's storms and emerge stronger, wiser, and more resilient than before. This chapter delves into nurturing resilience, exploring how to develop resilience in the face of adversity, learning from setbacks and failures, and building emotional strength and perseverance.

Developing Resilience in the Face of Adversity

Resilience is not the absence of adversity but rather the ability to bounce back. It is the capacity to adapt in the face of challenges, to find strength in adversity, and to emerge from difficult situations with renewed determination and resolve.

One way to develop resilience is by cultivating a growth mindset. Embrace challenges as opportunities for growth, view setbacks as temporary, and believe in your ability to overcome obstacles. By reframing adversity as a chance to learn, grow, and evolve, you empower yourself to face life's challenges with courage and resilience.

Another critical aspect of developing resilience is fostering a sense of self-efficacy. Believe in your ability to influence outcomes, take proactive steps to overcome obstacles, and seek support when needed. By cultivating a sense of agency and empowerment, you build the resilience necessary to navigate life's ups and downs with grace and resilience.

Learning from Setbacks and Failures

Setbacks and failures are not signs of weakness but opportunities for growth and learning. They provide valuable insights into our strengths and weaknesses, highlight areas for improvement, and serve as catalysts for personal growth and development.

Instead of viewing setbacks as roadblocks, see them as stepping stones to success. Embrace failure as a natural part of the learning process, extract lessons from your experiences, and use them to inform your future actions. By adopting a mindset of curiosity and resilience, you transform setbacks into opportunities for growth and self-discovery.

One effective strategy for learning from setbacks and failures is the practice of reflection. Take time to analyze your experiences, identify patterns and trends, and pinpoint areas for improvement. By approaching failure with curiosity and self-reflection, you uncover valuable insights that propel you towards greater resilience and success.

Building Emotional Strength and Perseverance

Emotional strength and perseverance are the resilience, providing the inner fortitude necessary to weather life's storms and emerge stronger on the other side. Building emotional strength requires a willingness to acknowledge and process difficult emotions, cultivate self-compassion, and develop healthy coping mechanisms.

One way to build emotional strength is by practising self-care. Make time for activities that nourish your mind, body, and soul, such as exercise, meditation, and spending time with loved ones. Prioritize your emotional well-being, set boundaries, and seek support when needed. By nurturing yourself, you build the emotional resilience necessary to navigate life's challenges with grace and resilience.

Perseverance is the ability to persist in the face of adversity and to keep moving forward despite obstacles and setbacks. Cultivate perseverance by setting realistic goals, breaking them down into manageable steps, and staying focused on your vision. Celebrate your successes, no matter how small, and remain committed to your journey, knowing that every step forward brings you closer to your goals.

In nurturing resilience, we cultivate the strength, courage, and perseverance necessary to navigate life's challenges with grace and resilience. By developing resilience in the face of adversity, learning from setbacks and failures, and building emotional strength and perseverance, we unlock the power to overcome obstacles, embrace change, and thrive in the face of adversity.

"Resilience is not about avoiding adversity, but about rising stronger after each fall." - Unknown.

"In the storm of life, resilience is the anchor that keeps us grounded and the sail that propels us forward." - Unknown.

"Failure is not the opposite of success; it's a stepping stone to success. Embrace, learn from, and grow stronger." - Unknown.

"Strength does not come from winning. Your struggles develop your strengths. When you go through hardships and decide not to surrender, that is strength." - Arnold Schwarzenegger.

"Resilience is the capacity to adapt to change, to bounce back from setbacks, and to keep moving forward with hope and determination." - Unknown.

Chapter 4:

Cultivating Self-Discovery

Embarking on a journey of self-discovery is kin to setting sail on uncharted waters, where every wave promises new insights, revelations, and self-awareness. This chapter will delve into the art of cultivating self-discovery, exploring how to embark on a journey of self-awareness, exploring passions, strengths, and values, and uncovering hidden potentials and talents.

Embarking on a Journey of Self-Awareness

Imagine a traveller setting out on a voyage to distant lands, armed with nothing but a compass and a thirst for adventure. Similarly, embarking on a journey of self-awareness requires courage, curiosity, and a willingness to explore the depths of your being. Self-awareness is the foundation upon which personal growth is built. It is the ability to recognize your thoughts, emotions, and behaviours without judgment and to gain insight into your motivations, fears, and aspirations. By embarking on a journey of self-awareness, you peel back the layers of conditioning and expectation, revealing the true essence of who you are.

One way to cultivate self-awareness is through mindfulness practices such as meditation, journaling, and introspection. Take time daily to pause, reflect, and connect with your innermost thoughts and feelings. You gain clarity, insight, and a deeper understanding of yourself and your place in the world by tuning into your inner landscape.

Exploring Passions, Strengths, and Values

Just as a gardener tends to their garden, nurturing the seeds of potential, so must we tend to the garden of our souls, cultivating our passions, strengths, and values with care and intention.

Exploring passions involves exploring activities, hobbies, and interests that ignite your curiosity and bring you joy. Pay attention to the activities that make time stand still, energize and inspire you, and align with your deepest values and aspirations. By exploring your passions, you tap into a wellspring of creativity, purpose, and fulfilment.

Identifying strengths is about recognizing your innate talents, abilities, and qualities that set you apart. Reflect on the tasks and activities that come naturally to you, the areas where you excel, and the qualities that others admire in you. By acknowledging your strengths, you cultivate a sense of confidence, resilience, and self-efficacy that propels you towards success and fulfilment.

Clarifying values involves reflecting on the principles, beliefs, and ideals that guide your decisions and actions. Consider what matters most to you, what you stand for, and what you are willing to sacrifice for. By aligning your actions with your values, you create a sense of integrity, authenticity, and purpose that infuses every aspect of your life with meaning and significance.

Uncovering Hidden Potentials and Talents

Like precious gems buried beneath the surface, hidden potentials and talents lie waiting to be unearthed and polished to brilliance. Uncovering these hidden treasures requires curiosity, exploration, and a willingness to embrace the unknown.

One way to uncover hidden potentials and talents is through experimentation and exploration. Step outside your comfort zone, try new experiences and challenge yourself to learn and grow. Pay attention to the activities that spark your curiosity, make you lose track of time, and leave you feeling energized and alive. You unlock doors to untapped potential and undiscovered talents by embracing new opportunities.

Another way to uncover hidden potentials and talents is through feedback and reflection. Seek input from trusted friends, mentors, and colleagues who can offer insights into your strengths, weaknesses, and areas for growth. Reflect on your past experiences, successes, and failures, and look for patterns and themes that point towards your unique gifts and talents. By listening to the wisdom of others and tuning into your inner voice, you uncover hidden potentials and skills that have been lying dormant within you, waiting to be awakened and unleashed upon the world.

In cultivating self-discovery, we embark on a journey of exploration and adventure, seeking to uncover the depths of our being and the richness of our potential. By embarking on a journey of self-awareness, exploring passions, strengths, and values, and uncovering hidden potentials and talents, we unlock the keys to a life of meaning, purpose, and fulfilment.

"The journey of self-discovery begins with the courage to explore the depths of your soul." - Unknown.

"In the garden of your soul, cultivate the seeds of self-awareness, water them with curiosity, and watch as they bloom into the flowers of wisdom." - Unknown.

"True self-discovery is not about finding yourself, but creating yourself anew with each passing moment." - Unknown.

"Your passions, strengths, and values are the compass that guides you on the journey of self-discovery. Listen to their whispers and follow their lead." - Unknown.

"Hidden within you are treasures waiting to be unearthed, talents longing to be discovered. Embrace the journey of self-discovery and unlock the magic within." - Unknown.

Chapter 5:

Pruning Limiting Beliefs

In the garden of the mind, limiting beliefs are like tangled weeds, choking out the sunlight of potential and stifling the growth of our dreams. This chapter will dig into the art of pruning limiting beliefs, exploring how to overcome self-doubt and fear, identify and challenge limiting beliefs, and cultivate a positive and empowering belief system.

Overcoming Self-Doubt and Fear

Imagine a young sapling reaching for the sky with trembling branches, unsure of its ability to withstand the storms that rage around it. Similarly, overcoming self-doubt and fear requires courage, resilience, and a willingness to confront the shadows that lurk within.

A student friend, Sarah, is a talented artist who dreams of sharing her work with the world but is plagued by self-doubt and fear of rejection. Despite the whispers of doubt that echo in her mind, Sarah decides to take a leap of faith and showcase her paintings at a local art exhibition.

As the day of the exhibition arrives, Sarah feels her heart pounding in her chest, her palms slick with sweat. But as she watches the admiring glances of the visitors, listens to the words of praise from fellow artists, and feels the swell of pride in her chest, she realizes that her self-doubt is nothing more than a shadow, quickly dispelled by the light of her courage.

Identifying and Challenging Limiting Beliefs

Limiting beliefs are like invisible chains, holding us back from reaching our full potential and keeping us tethered to the familiar shores of mediocrity. Identifying and challenging these beliefs is the first step towards breaking free from their grip and embracing the boundless possibilities that lie beyond.

Another story is of my close friend David, a successful executive who dreams of starting his own business but is held back by the belief that he is not intelligent or capable enough to succeed. Through introspection and reflection, David realizes that this belief is a relic of his past, a remnant of childhood insecurities that no longer serve him.

With determination and resolve, David challenges his limiting beliefs, seeking mentors, reading books, taking action and surrounding himself with people who believe in his potential. As he takes small steps towards his goal, each success becomes a brick in the foundation of a new belief system, one built on confidence, resilience, and unwavering self-belief. If you are in the position of David, I want to assure you that it is possible to go after your dreams and achieve them. Let go of everything and start today by taking action.

Cultivating a Positive and Empowering Belief System

Just as a gardener tends to her plants, nurturing them with care and attention, so must we tend to the garden of our minds, cultivating a positive and empowering belief system that nourishes our dreams and fuels our ambitions.

Maya is a young family member who dreams of pursuing a music career but is held back by the belief that she is not talented enough to succeed. Through daily affirmations, visualization techniques, and surrounding herself with supportive friends and family, Maya begins to plant the seeds of a new belief system rooted in positivity, possibility, and unwavering self-confidence.

As Maya's belief in herself grows, so does her ability to overcome obstacles, navigate setbacks, and stay true to her vision. With each passing day, she watches as the garden of her mind blooms with the vibrant colours of hope, resilience, and limitless potential.

In pruning limiting beliefs, we free ourselves from the shackles of self-doubt and fear and embrace the boundless potential that lies within. By overcoming self-doubt and fear, identifying and challenging limiting beliefs, and cultivating a positive and empowering belief system, we unlock the doors to a life of limitless possibility, joy, and fulfilment.

"Limiting beliefs are like weeds in the garden of your mind. Remove them, and watch your potential bloom." - Unknown.

"Courage is not the absence of fear, but the triumph over it. Prune your limiting beliefs and let your bravery shine." - Nelson Mandela.

"Your beliefs shape your reality. Prune away the negative, and watch as your world transforms." - Unknown.

"The only limits that exist are the ones you place on yourself. Prune away self-doubt and watch your potential soar." - Unknown.

"Believe in yourself and all that you are. Prune away the doubts, and watch as you blossom into your fullest potential." - Unknown.

Chapter 6:

Fostering Growth Relationships

In the landscape of personal growth, relationships are the fertile soil where our aspirations take root and flourish. This chapter will explore the art of fostering growth relationships, nurturing supportive and uplifting connections, building healthy boundaries and communication skills, and surrounding oneself with positive influences.

Nurturing Supportive and Uplifting Connections

Nurturing supportive and uplifting connections means actively fostering relationships that provide emotional support, encouragement, and positive growth. This involves more than just having friends or acquaintances; it requires intentionality and effort to cultivate deeper, more meaningful connections.

These connections offer a wealth of benefits for personal growth including:

Emotional Support: They provide a safe space to share your joys, sorrows and struggles, knowing you'll be listened to and accepted without judgment. This can help you navigate difficult times and build resilience.

Encouragement and Motivation: Supportive connections offer positive reinforcement, believing in you and your goals. This can boost your confidence, provide inspiration, and help you stay motivated during challenges.

Feedback and Growth: Honest and constructive feedback from trusted connections can help you identify areas for improvement and develop personally and professionally.

Sense of Belonging: Knowing you're part of a supportive community fosters a sense of belonging and reduces feelings of isolation, contributing to overall well-being.

New Perspectives: Interacting with people from diverse backgrounds and experiences exposes you to new ideas and ways of thinking, broadening your perspective and understanding of the world.

Increased Happiness and Well-being: Strong, positive connections have been linked to increased happiness, reduced stress, and improved physical and mental health.

How to Nurture Supportive and Uplifting Connections:

Focus on Quality, Not Quantity: Prioritize investing time and effort in developing deeper connections with a few individuals rather than having many superficial ones.

Be a Good Listener: Show genuine interest in others, actively listen to their experiences, and offer empathy and support.

Practice Communication: Share openly and honestly, express your feelings, and be receptive to feedback.

Offer Help and Support: Be there for others in times of need, offer assistance, and celebrate their successes.

Engage in Shared Activities: Spend time together doing things you both enjoy, fostering shared experiences and strengthening the bond.

Respect and Appreciate: Show appreciation for your connections, acknowledging their value in your life.

Be Patient and Consistent: Building strong connections takes time and effort. Be patient, nurture them consistently, and remember that even small gestures can make a difference.

Building Healthy Boundaries and Communication Skills

Healthy relationships are built on a foundation of mutual respect, trust, and understanding. Creating healthy boundaries and communication skills is essential for fostering growth relationships that withstand the test of time and adversity.

About my own brother's story, Ben and Sarah are a couple navigating the challenges of a long-distance relationship. Through open and honest communication, they establish clear boundaries around their needs, expectations, and priorities, ensuring their relationship remains strong and resilient despite distance.

As Ben and Sarah learn to communicate effectively and set boundaries honouring their needs, their connection deepens and grows stronger daily. By prioritizing open dialogue and mutual respect, they create a safe and supportive space where their love can thrive and flourish.

Surrounding oneself with Positive Influences

Just as a flower turns towards the sun to bask in its warmth and light, we must also seek out positive influences that nourish our spirits and inspire us to reach for the stars.

Surrounding yourself with positive influences can be achieved in several ways throughout your personal growth journey:

Reflect on qualities: What values, attitudes, and characteristics do you appreciate in others? Consider individuals who inspire, motivate, and support you.

Assess your current circle: Evaluate your existing relationships. Who uplifts you and aligns with your goals? Are there negative influences you might limit contact with?

Expand your network:

Join communities: Seek out groups, clubs, or online forums aligned with your interests and goals.

Attend events: Participate in workshops, conferences, or meetups related to your personal development aspirations.

Volunteer: Engaging in meaningful activities can connect you with like-minded individuals who share your values.

Deepen existing connections:

Initiate quality time: Invest in deeper conversations and shared activities with individuals who positively impact you.

Practice active listening: Show genuine interest in their lives, offer support, and celebrate their achievements.

Be open and vulnerable: Share your authentic self and be receptive to their feedback and perspectives.

Set boundaries with negativity:

Recognize the impact: Notice how certain individuals drain your energy or hinder your progress.

Limit exposure: Minimize contact with those who are judgmental, critical, or bring negativity into your life.

Directly communicate: If possible, have honest conversations about their impact and set healthy boundaries.

Become a positive influence yourself:

Spread kindness and empathy: Contribute positively to the lives of others, offering support and encouragement.

Celebrate diversity: Embrace different perspectives and experiences, fostering a welcoming and inclusive environment.

Lead by example: Live by the values you cherish and demonstrate the characteristics you seek in others.

Remember, surrounding yourself with positive influences is a continuous process. It requires introspection, effort, and, sometimes, letting go of unhealthy connections. But by actively cultivating supportive and uplifting relationships, you create a powerful force that can propel you towards your personal growth goals and enrich your life overall.

"Surround yourself with those who see the greatness within you and help you manifest it." - Unknown

"In the garden of life, relationships are the flowers that bloom with love, nurture, and care." - Unknown.

"Healthy boundaries are the key to maintaining relationships that uplift and inspire." - Unknown.

"Communication is the bridge that connects hearts, minds, and souls in the journey of growth and connection." - Unknown

"Choose relationships that water your soul, nurture your spirit, and help you grow into the best version of yourself." - Unknown

Chapter 7

Harvesting Gratitude and Mindfulness

Welcome to the lush fields of gratitude and mindfulness, where the fruits of awareness and appreciation await to be savoured. In this chapter, we embark on an adventure into the heart of gratitude and mindfulness, exploring their transformative power as catalysts for personal growth. We'll delve into cultivating gratitude, embracing mindfulness, and finding joy in the simple moments that make life extraordinary.

Cultivating Gratitude as a Catalyst for Personal Growth

Cultivating gratitude can be a powerful tool for personal growth in many ways. Here are some steps you can take to achieve it.

Start small and build a habit:

Morning practice: Begin your day with a simple appreciation for something small, like your warm bed, a cup of coffee, or the sunrise.

Gratitude journal: Spend 5-10 minutes each day writing down 3-5 things you're grateful for. Be specific and reflect on why you appreciate them.

Gratitude jar: Write down things you're grateful for on pieces of paper, fold them up, and put them in a jar. Periodically revisit and read them for a boost.

Expand your scope of gratitude

Appreciating experiences: Go beyond material things and acknowledge the people, moments, and experiences that enrich your life.

Expressing gratitude: Say "thank you" to others, write gratitude letters, or even offer compliments. Witnessing the positive impact on others deepens your gratitude.

Shifting perspective: Reframe challenges as opportunities for learning and growth. See setbacks as stepping stones on your journey.

Integrate gratitude into daily life:

Mindfulness practices: Pause throughout the day to appreciate your surroundings, your senses, and even simple tasks.

Random acts of kindness: Do something good for someone else without expecting anything in return. Witnessing the joy you bring others fuels your own sense of gratitude.

Celebrating small wins: Acknowledge and celebrate your achievements, no matter how small. This reinforces a positive mindset and fosters appreciation for your progress.

Remember

Consistency is key: Like any skill, cultivating gratitude takes practice. Stick with it, even when you don't feel like it.

Focus on the positive: Train your mind to focus on the good things in your life, rather than dwelling on negativity.

Be specific: The more specific you are about what you're grateful for, the deeper your gratitude will be.

Practising Mindfulness and Living in the Present Moment

One of my co-workers, Abby, is a restless soul plagued by worries about the future and regrets about the past. Through mindfulness, she learns to anchor herself in the present moment, letting go of anxieties and regrets that weigh her down.

She attains to the present moment's sights, sounds, and sensations with each mindful breath. Abby savours the taste of her morning coffee, feels the sun's warmth on her skin, and marvels at the beauty of a flower in bloom. In the stillness of mindfulness, she discovers a profound sense of peace and clarity, allowing her to navigate life's challenges with grace and poise.

Finding Joy and Fulfilment in Everyday Experiences

Here are some ways you can achieve this:

Practice mindfulness: Pay attention to the present moment without judgment. Notice the sights, sounds, smells, and sensations around you. This helps you appreciate the little things often overlooked.
Reframe negativity: Instead of dwelling on the shortcomings of a situation, try to find the positive aspects. Look for opportunities to learn and grow from challenges.

Cultivate curiosity: Approach everyday experiences with a beginner's mind. Ask questions, explore new things, and be open to wonder and discovery. Engage in activities that bring you joy:

Pursue hobbies and interests: Make time for activities you genuinely enjoy, whether reading, music, drawing, sports, or anything else that sparks your passion.

Connect with nature: Spend time outdoors, immerse yourself in natural beauty, and appreciate the peace and tranquillity it offers.

Connect with loved ones: Share meaningful experiences with friends and family. Laughing and connection can be deeply fulfilling.

Practice gratitude: Regularly acknowledge the good things in your life, both big and small. This cultivates a positive outlook and appreciation for everyday experiences.

Challenge yourself and step outside your comfort zone:

Learn new skills: Take a class, read a book, or try something you've always wanted to do but were afraid to. Learning new things keeps your mind sharp and opens up new possibilities.

Take on new challenges: Volunteer for a cause you care about, participate in a competition or set a personal goal for yourself. Overcoming challenges builds confidence and resilience.

Help others: Offer your time, skills, or resources to those in need. Giving back to the community can be incredibly rewarding and connect you to something bigger than yourself.

Be present and engaged:

Put away distractions: When you're engaged in an activity, give it your full attention. Minimize distractions like phones or electronics to be truly present in the moment.
Savour the experience: Slow down and pay attention to the details of your experiences. Take time to appreciate each activity's sights, sounds, smells, and feelings.
Reflect on your experiences: Take some time each day to reflect on what you did and how it made you feel. This allows you to learn from your experiences and appreciate their impact on your growth.

Remember

Personal growth is a journey, not a destination: Don't be discouraged if you don't find joy and fulfilment in every experience. Be patient, experiment, and focus on progress over perfection.
It's all about you: What brings you joy and fulfilment will be unique. Pay attention to your own needs and interests and tailor your approach accordingly.
Celebrate your progress: Acknowledge and celebrate your successes, no matter how small. This reinforces your positive efforts and motivates you to keep growing.

By incorporating these practices into your daily life, you can unlock the potential for joy and fulfilment in even the most ordinary experiences, ultimately leading to personal growth and a more meaningful life.

"Gratitude turns what we have into enough, and mindfulness turns moments into blessings." - Unknown.

"In the garden of life, gratitude is the water that nourishes the seeds of joy and mindfulness is the sunlight that helps them grow." - Unknown.

"When we cultivate gratitude and mindfulness, we harvest a life rich in abundance, peace, and contentment." - Unknown.

"Mindfulness is the art of being present. Gratitude is the art of noticing. Together, they create a masterpiece of a life well-lived." - Unknown.

"In the tapestry of life, gratitude and mindfulness are the threads that weave together moments of beauty, wonder, and joy." - Unknown.

Chapter 8:

Sustaining Growth and Integration

As you reach the final chapter of this book, you will stand on the precipice of transformation, poised to integrate the lessons learned and the growth experienced into the fabric of your daily lives. This chapter explores the art of sustaining growth and integration, integrating personal growth into daily life, creating sustainable habits and routines, and embracing lifelong learning and continuous development.

Integrating Personal Growth into Daily Life

Integrating personal growth into your daily life isn't about drastic changes but mindful, consistent actions that lead to lasting progress. Here are some ideas to get you started.

Mindfulness and Self-Care:

Start small: Begin with 5-minute mindfulness exercises like meditation or deep breathing.

Prioritize sleep: Aim for 7-8 hours to boost energy and cognitive function.

Move your body: Find activities you enjoy, like walking, dancing, or yoga.

Nourish yourself: Eat balanced meals, stay hydrated, and limit processed foods.

Practice gratitude: Reflect on things you're thankful for through journaling or mental affirmations.

Growth Mindset and Learning:

Embrace challenges: See them as opportunities to learn and grow.

Read books or articles: Explore interesting topics, expanding your knowledge and perspective.

Listen to podcasts: Learn on the go while commuting, exercising, or doing chores.

Take online courses: Develop new skills or deepen existing ones at your own pace.

Reflection and Accountability:

Journaling: Reflect on your day, successes, challenges, and areas for improvement.

Gratitude journaling: Reflect on things you're grateful for to boost happiness and positivity.

Track your progress: Monitor your goals and celebrate milestones, big or small.

Seek feedback: Ask for constructive criticism from trusted individuals to identify areas for growth.

Michael, my classmate and recent graduate, has spent the past year immersing himself in self-improvement books, seminars, and workshops.

Despite his newfound knowledge and insights, Michael struggles to translate his learnings into meaningful action in his day-to-day life.

Through reflection and introspection, Michael begins to identify areas where he can integrate his growth journey into his daily routine. He sets aside time each morning for meditation and journaling, practices gratitude throughout the day, and engages in regular self-reflection to track his progress and identify areas for growth.

As Michael integrates personal growth into his daily life, he discovers that transformation is not a destination but a journey that unfolds in the small moments of everyday living. With each conscious choice and intentional action, he moves closer to becoming the best version of himself, one step at a time.

Creating Sustainable Habits and Routines

My best friend Jacqueline is a busy professional balancing the demands of work, family, and personal life. She recognizes the importance of creating sustainable habits and routines that support her growth and well-being but struggles to find the time and energy to do so.

Through experimentation and trial and error, she identifies small changes she can make to her daily routines that greatly impact her overall well-being. She starts meal prepping on Sundays to ensure she eats nutritious meals throughout the week, incorporates short bursts of exercise into her daily schedule, and sets aside time each evening for relaxation and self-care.

As Jacqueline commits to her new habits and routines, she discovers a sense of empowerment and control over her life. With each healthy choice she makes, she reinforces her commitment to her growth journey and lays the foundation for a sustainable and fulfilling future.

From my friend's story, I want to inform you that creating sustainable habits is a journey, not a destination. Be patient, experiment, and find what works best for you. With consistent effort and the right approach, you can build habits and routines that support your personal growth and help you reach your full potential.

Embracing Lifelong Learning and Continuous Development

Maya, my mom's sister, is a retiree who has spent a lifetime dedicated to learning and personal growth. Despite her many accomplishments and achievements, Maya recognizes that there is always more to discover and explore on the journey of self-discovery.

Through curiosity and a thirst for knowledge, she embraces lifelong learning as a cornerstone of her growth journey. She enrols in online courses, attends workshops and seminars, and seeks opportunities to engage with new ideas and perspectives. With each new insight she gains, Maya deepens her understanding of herself and the world around her, and her journey of growth and discovery unfolds.

Reflecting on her life, she realizes that personal growth is not a destination but a way of being, a commitment to embracing the unknown and stepping outside her comfort zone. With each new chapter, she discovers that the journey of growth is never-ending and that the possibilities for learning and development are limitless.

In sustaining growth and integration, we honour the journey we have embarked upon and commit to nurturing our growth and well-being in the days, weeks, and years to come. By integrating personal growth into daily life, creating sustainable habits and routines, and embracing lifelong learning and continuous development, we lay the foundation for a life of purpose, meaning, and fulfilment.

"Integration is the key that unlocks the door to sustained growth, allowing our learnings to become the fabric of our daily lives." - Unknown.

"Sustainable habits are the building blocks of a life well-lived, paving the way for growth and transformation to flourish." - Unknown.

"In the journey of continuous development, the path is never-ending, and the possibilities for growth are boundless." - Unknown.

"True growth is not measured by how high we climb, but by how deeply we integrate our learnings into the rhythm of our daily lives." - Unknown.

"Lifelong learning is the fuel that propels us forward on the journey of growth, igniting our curiosity and expanding our horizons." - Unknown.

Conclusion:

Unlock Your Potential: The Best Guide to Personal Growth Quotes and Ideas Book

In the journey of personal growth, you have explored the depths of the potential, embraced the challenges of self-discovery, and discovered the transformative power of gratitude, mindfulness, and continuous learning Remember that the path to unlocking our potential is not a destination but a way of being—a commitment to growth, resilience, and self-discovery in every moment of our lives.

Each chapter has offered valuable insights and practical strategies for cultivating a life of purpose, meaning, and fulfilment. From nurturing supportive relationships to embracing mindfulness and gratitude, I hope you have learned that personal growth is not a solitary pursuit but a collaborative journey—one that is enriched by the connections we forge, the lessons we know, and the experiences we share.

As you reflect on the wisdom shared within these pages, I encourage you to embrace the power of intention and the possibility of personal growth. Remember that you hold the seeds of greatness, waiting to be nurtured and cultivated. Trust in your journey, believe in your potential and know that each step brings you closer to the life you envision.

In the tapestry of life, you are the weaver of your destiny, the architect of your dreams. Let gratitude be your compass, mindfulness your guide, and continuous learning your companion on the journey of growth and self-discovery. May you find joy in the journey, strength in the challenges, and beauty in the moments of everyday living.

As you close this book, remember that the most incredible adventure lies not in reaching the summit but in embracing the climb. Embrace the journey, cherish the lessons, and celebrate the person you are becoming. In unlocking your potential, you unleash the boundless possibilities that lie within you—and in doing so, you inspire others to do the same.

Thank you for embarking on this journey of growth and exploration. May your path be illuminated by the light of possibility, and may you continue to unlock your potential with courage, grace, and an unwavering belief in the power of your dreams.

I would be glad to see your review if you have made it to the end and had any value from this book; thank you.

If you want to know more about me visit:
https://www.digitalsuccesspay.com/

Printed in Great Britain
by Amazon